W9-CKH-123

SEA SLIME

It's Eeuwy, Gooey, and Under the Sea

by Ellen Prager
illustrated by Shennen Bersani

Under the sea, there is something gooey. It slips, slides, and sticks. Lots of ocean animals have it. They use it to go fast and find food. Some undersea creatures even use it to avoid becoming someone else's lunch.

It's SEA SLIME!

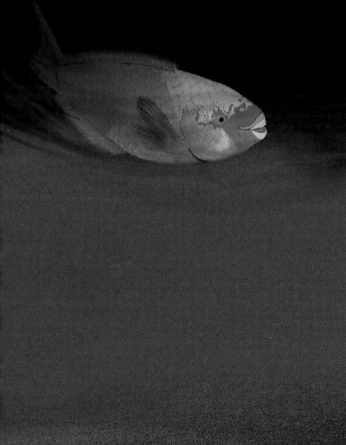

The jellyfish drifts slowly in the sea. It is shaped like an umbrella with stringy, stinging tentacles and long, frilly, feeding arms that hang down. The jellyfish is not really a swimmer; it just pumps its way up then sinks back down.

This creature does not just use ocean goo. Its whole body is see-through SLIME.

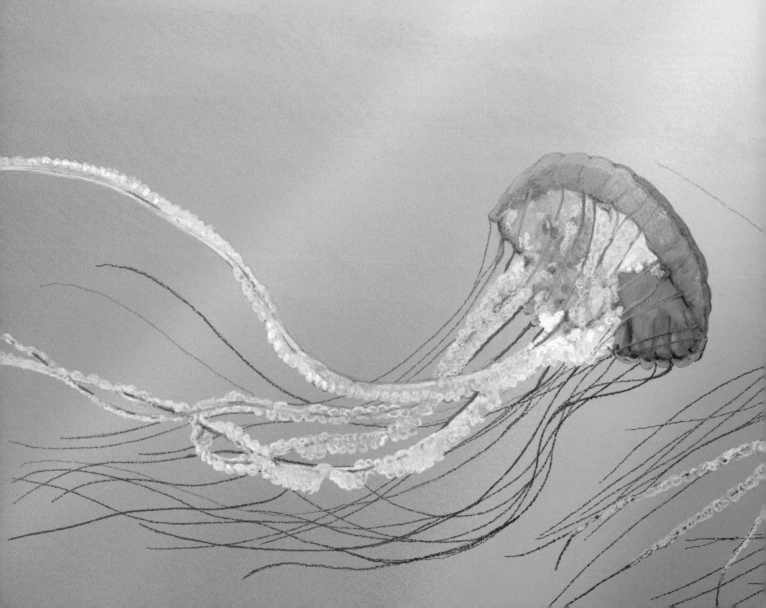

Many snails live in the ocean. Some snails swim, some float, and others crawl across the seafloor.

The sea slug mainly crawls. It is a snail with no shell. Sea slugs are very colorful creatures; some have stripes and others wear polka dots. They move slowly over sand, climb up corals, and tiptoe across ropes of algae.

To go faster, a sea slug travels over its own slippery goo. It slithers, slips, and slides across SLIME.

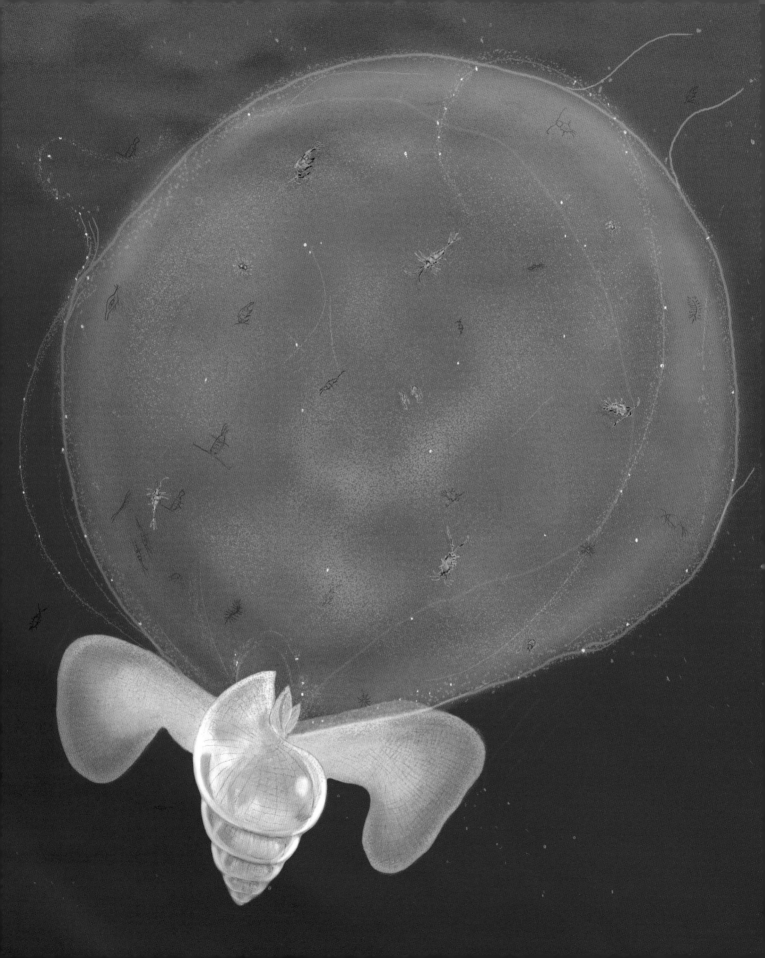

Swimming snails use fins like wings to fly through the sea. They are called pteropods or sea butterflies. Some sea butterflies have shells, while others do not.

They have a strange and sticky way to find food. Sea butterflies blow a bubble of mucus like a parachute of sticky goo. Drifting bits and pieces of tiny creatures get stuck to their floating bubble. For a yummy feast, these swimming snails slurp up their bubble of SLIME.

In the sea, there is another snail that floats.
The violet snail has a spiraling purple shell.

It makes a raft out of bubbles to stay afloat.
They are bubbles of purple SLIME.

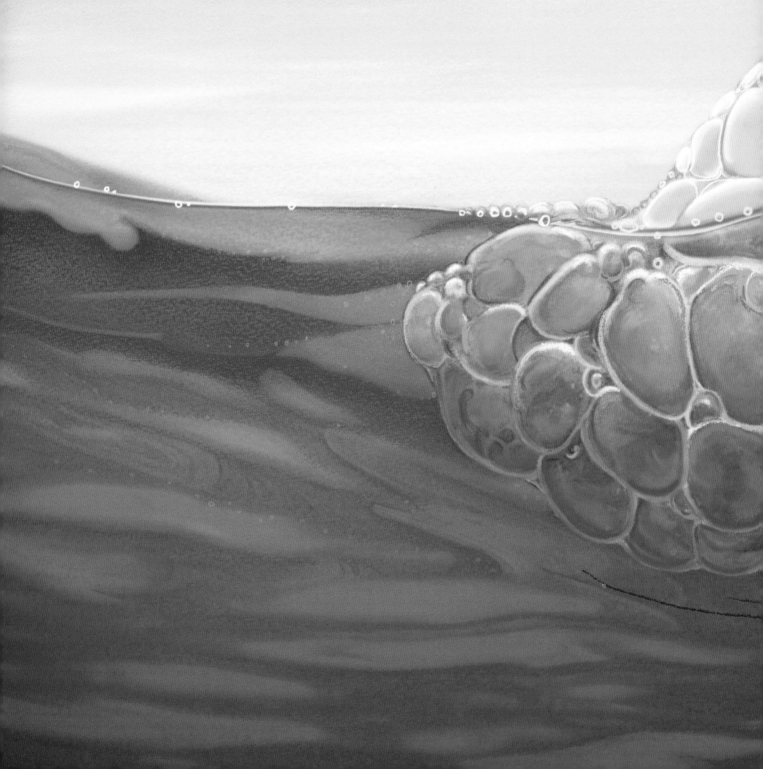

Fish use undersea goo, too. In the coral reef lives the colorful parrotfish. During the day, it nibbles algae and scrapes seaweed off of rocks.

At night, some parrotfish find a safe, cozy place to sleep. They nestle down in holes in the reef and then do something very special. For protection while they are sleeping, these fish create a cocoon of goo. It is their very own blanket of SLIME.

The cute clownfish has a partner under the sea. The clownfish swims and sleeps in the stinging arms of an anemone for protection. But why doesn't the clownfish get stung?

A layer of goo on the fish prevents it from getting hurt. The clownfish wears a wetsuit of SLIME.

Is it a snake? Is it an eel? No, but this fish looks a little bit like both. The hagfish is a long, skinny, and slippery fish. It lives on the bottom, deep in the sea.

When danger comes to call, the hagfish makes undersea goo! Lots of goo! The hagfish covers its enemies in sticky, slippery SLIME.

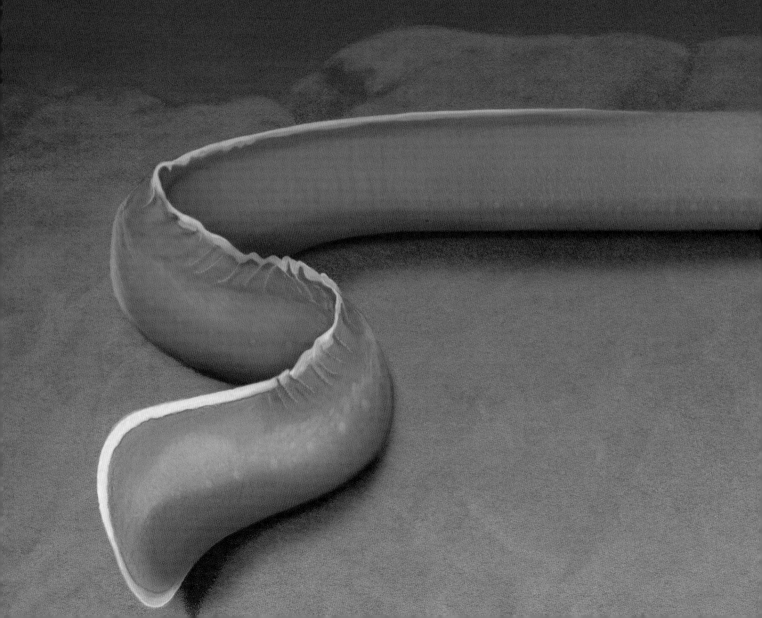

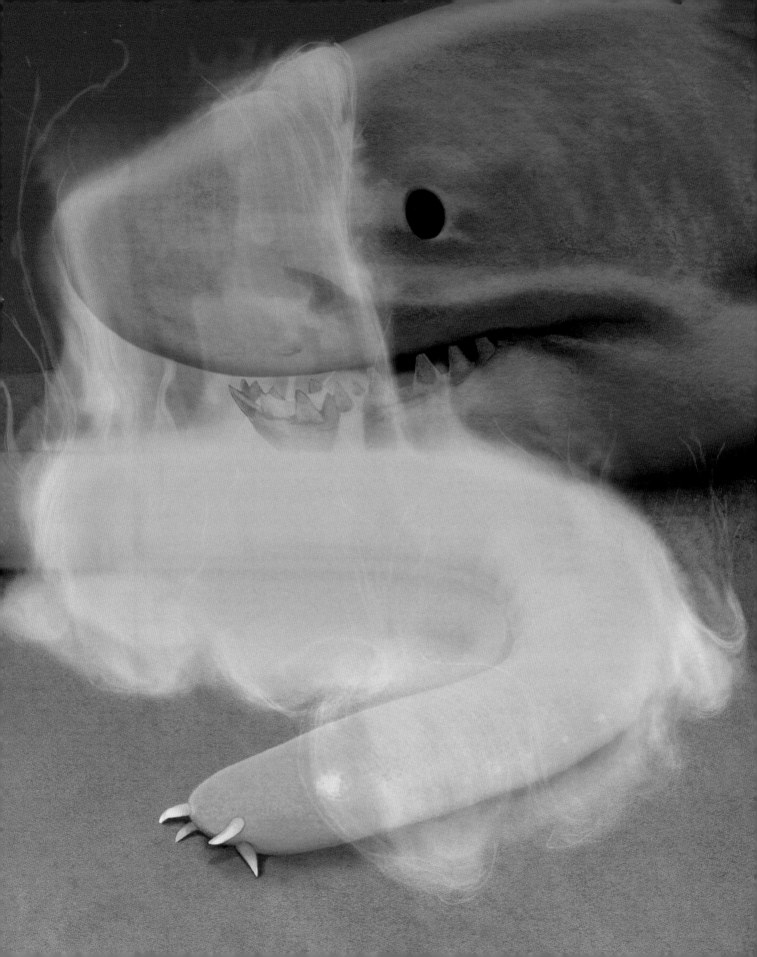

These undersea creatures also look like snakes. They are long, have a pointy snout, and very sharp teeth. But don't worry, you are not a good meal for the moray eel. They like to eat things like small crabs, worms, octopi, and fishes.

Moray eels don't have scales like fish. Instead, their bodies are coated with slippery goo. They wear an

The squid is an amazing ocean animal. It has big eyes, eight arms, and two tentacles. It can swim slowly or go fast like a jet. The squid can hover like a helicopter and change its color super fast.

If another animal tries to eat the squid, it has another trick up its eight arms. The squid can squirt out inky goo and create an undersea smokescreen of SLIME.

Deep in the dark sea swims a really weird creature. It looks like a plump, velvet football with a large head, eight arms, two tentacles, and two big balls for eyes. The vampire squid is one of the ocean's strangest animals. It can even shoot beads of glowing goo from the tips of its arms! The vampire squid has an eight-armed squirt gun that fires SLIME.

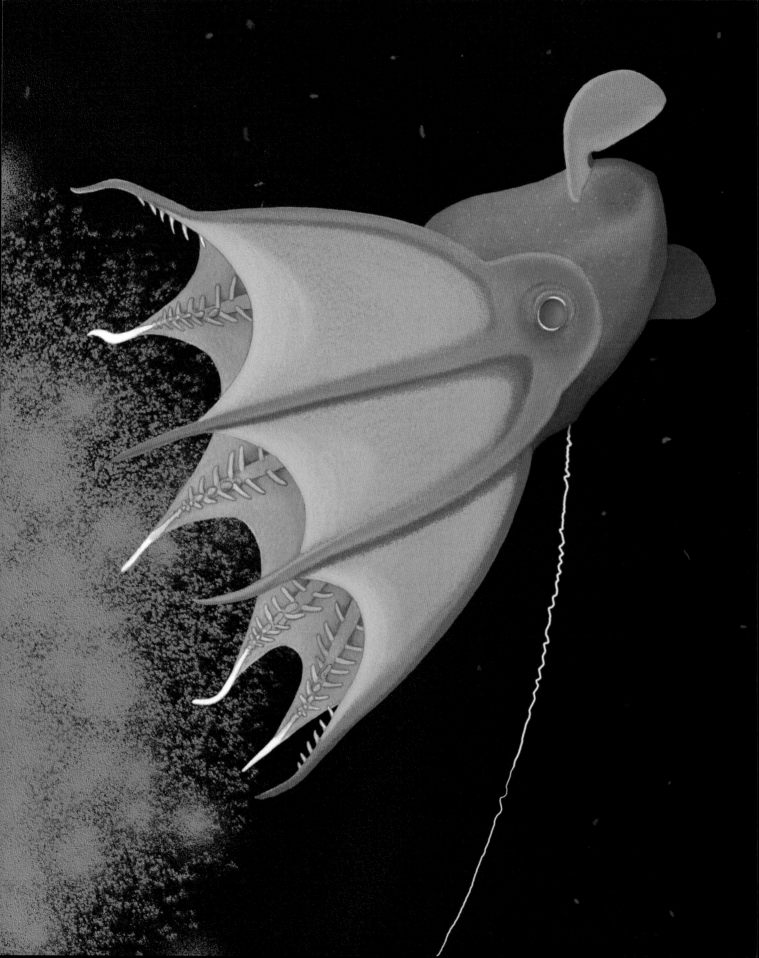

They are not fish or squids or snails. They look a lot like rocks sitting on the seafloor. But corals are much, much more. They are a colony of small animals called polyps. The coral polyp is mostly just a ring of tentacles around a stomach. As tiny animals drift by, the polyp captures and eats them.

Corals also have a very special way to wash off what lands on top of them. They make slippery goo that slides off their sides. Corals wash with SLIME.

It is very slippery, really gooey, and sometimes sticky. In the sea, SLIME comes in handy. If you lived in the ocean, you might have some too. Would you make a SLIME slide or have a SLIME squirt gun? Would you create a blanket of SLIME or use it to wash off dirt? Or how about blowing a bubble of SLIME as a net to capture your food? If you lived under the sea, how would you use your SLIME?

For Creative Minds

Slimy Animals True or False?

1. Slime is bad!

2. Corals are animals.

3. Jellyfish are fish.

4. Hagfish can bite through the skin of their prey.

5. In the ocean, all snails crawl on the sea floor.

6. Moray eels have scales like fish.

7. Some animals in the ocean also use slime as sunscreen.

8. The teeth of the parrotfish are fused together so they look like a parrot's beak.

9. Slime can help prevent animals in the ocean from getting sick.

10. Many sea slugs are brightly colored to scare off predators.

Answers: 1. False. In the ocean, sea creatures use slime in lots of ways that are helpful. 2. True. 3. False. Jellyfish are not fish, but their name makes it confusing. Jellyfish are related to corals. 4. False. Hagfish do not have jaws and only have small teeth on their tongues. They cannot bite through the skin or scales of fish. 5. False. The pteropods or sea butterflies spend their entire lives swimming in the water. Their foot has evolved into one or a pair of tiny, wing-like fins for swimming. 6. False. Moray eels' bodies are coated with slippery goo. 7. True. 8. True. 9. True. 10. True. Many sea slugs are brightly colored; this acts as a warning to predators. It is like a sign saying, "Don't eat me or you will be sorry."

Why Slime?

What are some reasons that YOU might want to use slime? How do those reasons compare to why animals use slime?

It is Slippery!

Which is easier and more fun to slide down, a wet or dry slide? The water makes the slide more slippery so you go down faster and smoother (and you don't get stuck). Slime makes it easier to travel over the sea floor or sand.

It is Sticky!

What would you use to trap bugs crawling on the floor, a regular piece of paper or one with glue on the surface?
The gluey one of course! Slime can be used like sticky paper or gooey bubble gum to capture things that crawl, float, or swim by.

It Floats!

If you blow air through a straw into a tall glass of water, where do the bubbles go?
They go up to the surface because air is lighter than water. Bubbles made of slime and air rises to the water's surface and help animals to stay afloat.

It Keeps Away Predators!

Shooting slime at your enemies is a good way to make them go away. Or you could fool them with a cloud of slime that looks like you, giving you a chance to slip away unnoticed.

It Protects!

Wrapping yourself in a blanket of mucus deters enemies. If you coated yourself with slime, not too many people would want to get very close. And, like the antibiotic ointment you put on cuts, slime keeps bad bacteria out.

It Cleans!

Which would work better to get mud and dirt off, a blast of air or a hose with soapy water?
Soap makes water slippery and sticky, almost like slime. Some ocean animals coat themselves with slime. When they get dirty, they just make some more slime and the old, grimy slime slides off. Slime is good for washing.

Lifestyles of the Wet and Slimy

sea anemone

Within the ocean there are many different types of habitats. These are the places or environments that animals call home.

A habitat can be as small as a single **sea anemone** or one blade of grass or as big as the **ocean's surface**, where the wind, sun, and waves meet.

sea surface

In the ocean, seaweed and algae grow where there is enough sunlight. Some undersea animals are grazers and feed on algae and seaweed, the ocean's plants.

Coral reefs are where colonies of coral polyps grow and live together. They typically like warm, clear water with plenty of sunlight.

Kelp beds are like towering underwater forests with lots of hiding places. Kelp is a fast-growing brown algae that lives in cold, rocky areas.

Sea grasses create undersea meadows in the shallow parts of the ocean. Lots of small fish, crabs, and other animals live among the blades of these ocean pastures.

coral reef

kelp bed

sea grass

twilight zone

As the ocean gets deeper, there is less and less sunlight. There is just a little bit of light in the area called the **twilight zone**.

In the **deep sea** there is no light. Animals that live here must find a way to adapt to and live in total darkness.

deep sea
no light at all

Animals in the ocean live in a variety of habitats. Many animals stay in their home habitats all their lives, but other creatures may swim or crawl from one habitat to another.

Make Your Own Slime—It's Fun and It's Messy

What You Will Need:
- box of cornstarch (16 oz.)
- measuring cup
- water
- food coloring (optional, but fun)
- large bowl
- large spoon and small hands
- newspaper, plastic tablecloth, or good cleaning supplies

Here's How:
- First, cover your workspace with newspaper or a plastic tablecloth.
- Measure 1/2 cup of water into a bowl. If you want to make colored slime, add food coloring to the water now.
- Measure 1 cup of cornstarch.
- Slowly add the cornstarch to the water in the bowl, mixing as you go.
- Add additional cornstarch until you have the thickness of slime you desire! Dive right in with your hands for better mixing and to test the slime factor.
- Dig in and feel the **SLIME!** How does it feel in your hands? Pass it back and forth, or drip it into the bowl—have some fun!
- When you are finished, put the slime in the trash. Do not dump the slime down the drain or you might have to call a plumber.

Food for thought:
- How would you describe your slime?
  - What does it look like?
  - What does it feel like?
- Are there things at school or around your house that might be slimy? If so, what?
- Why do you think those things might be slimy?
- What could you do with your slime?

While doing research for the illustrations, I flew into Monterey, CA, drove to Mystic, CT, and returned to Boston. I want to thank Jim Fuller at the Monterey Bay Aquarium, again. Jim and the aquarium staff opened their doors wide to me, allowed me to go behind the scenes, and truly helped make my illustrations possible. I've held squid, jellyfish, sea slugs, oh my! I also stopped by to see Astro and his slimy pals at the Mystic Aquarium, and I watched the Giant Ocean Tank be renovated at the New England Aquarium. My deepest thanks also go out to Alienor Fratoni. Ali traveled where I dare not go, circumventing the globe, emailing me photos of the ocean along her way. *Merci beaucoup*!—SB

Thanks to Kimberly B. Ritchie, Ph.D., Senior Scientist and Manager, Marine Microbiology Program at the Mote Marine Laboratory for reviewing this book for accuracy.

Library of Congress Cataloging-in-Publication Data

Prager, Ellen J., author.
  Sea slime : it's eeuwy, gooey and under the sea / by Ellen Prager ; illustrated by Shennen Bersani.
      pages cm
   Audience: 4-8.
   Audience: Grade K to 3.
   ISBN 978-1-62855-210-2 (English hardcover) -- ISBN 978-1-62855-219-5 (English pbk.) -- ISBN 978-1-62855-237-9 (English downloadable ebook) -- ISBN 978-1-62855-255-3 (English dual-language interactive ebook) -- ISBN 978-1-62855-228-7 (Spanish pbk.) -- ISBN 978-1-62855-246-1 (Spanish downloadable ebook) -- ISBN 978-1-62855-264-5 (Spanish dual-language interactive ebook)
1. Marine animals--Juvenile literature. 2. Mucous membrane--Juvenile literature. 3. Animal chemical defenses--Juvenile literature. I. Bersani, Shennen, illustrator. II. Title.
QL122.2.P73 2014
591.47--dc23
                                    2013036391

This title is also available in Spanish: *Mucosa marina: Es pegajosa, asquerosa y en el océano . . . fabulosa*

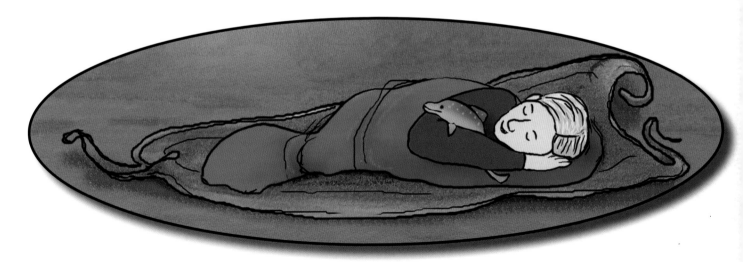

Lexile® Level: 730
key phrases for educators: animal adaptations, ocean habitat

Manufactured in China, December 2013
This product conforms to CPSIA 2008
First Printing

Sylvan Dell Publishing
Mt. Pleasant, SC 29464
www.SylvanDellPublishing.com